Real life
and fun
poetry

By Daniel Mitchell

Welcome to my book of poetry.

When I was a young child I had a poem written about me, by one of my teachers at school.

Ever since then, I have picked up in a great way with poems and, while some of my poems are purely for laughter, most of them have real meanings to them.

Examples of the poems include a wedding speech and a 40th speech.

Happy reading.

Introductory poem

A selection of poems
Most of them are true,
Some are about friends
Which involves some of you.

Some of them are about me
About my present and my past,
But I just love my poetry
And I write them very fast.

So enjoy reading my poetry
About my life and every need,
As I am sure most of this
Will give you an enjoyable read.

Jodi and Rich wedding day

I would like to say a massive "Thank you"
To everybody here,
For coming to the wedding of Rich and Jodi
My sister whom I love so dear.

I can still remember
Like it was yesterday,
When Jodi asked the question
"Will you give me away"?

When Jodi was a little girl
I used to act a fool,
I'd make her giggle in her buggy
When I was coming home from school.

Then as we got older
She used to make me swear,
By going through my clothes
And nicking what I wanted to wear.

Then as we reached adulthood
We kept a special bond,
The type that any family
Would be very fond.

Jodi met Rich and had children
Whom I do adore,
So when it comes to sisters
I could not ask for any more.

And today has been so lovely
It has gone without a hitch,
So I'd like to wish all the best
To both Jodi and Rich.

First year of Slimming World

I joined Slimming World in February
Feeling very fat,
And like all other diets
I thought I'd look a prat.

I know I am outnumbered
By the odd girl or maybe 2,
But they were all welcoming
Which definitely includes you.

You help us with our questions
You always lend your ear,
But when we have done well
You always give a cheer.

You do not embarrass us
When we gain an ounce (or maybe ten),
You just help us with our problems
So we don't do it again.

So I'd like to thank you once more
For all the help you share,
As it is so obvious
That you truly care.

Second year at Slimming World

My second year at Slimming World
Is almost at an end,
But I don't feel I have colleagues
As everyone is much more like a friend.

Those with whom I weigh each week
Are such a lovely crowd,
Some are very quiet
And some can be quite loud.

I would not have got this far
Without the class support,
And all the slimming secrets
Which I have been taught.

When I turn up on a Tuesday
I could not ask for any more,
Especially when I am 2 hours late
And get weighed in the corridor.

I do know (as a bloke)
I should give this next bit a miss,
But there are even times when I do think
"Does my bum look big in this"?

Where would we be right now
Especially someone like me,
Without all the help
From the wonderful Julie.

So we would like to thank you Julie
For so many slimming hours,
And from everyone here right now
Would you please accept these flowers.

The lucky 4 stone loss

Last week I weighed in Braintree
And I really cannot moan,
As I stepped onto the scales
And got my 4 stone.

When I received my award
The whole class gave a cheer,
And I really must admit
I even shed a tear.

To make things even better
I had one more surprise,
I tried on a pair of jeans
And dropped another size.

I really must admit
This really made my day,
As later on in the year
I give my beautiful sister away.

But I really must admit
I don't know what I'd do,
Without the help and support
From every one of you.

New year 2012

New year's eve is almost here
And I will be alone,
All I will have for company
Is every mobile phone.

I won't get a cuddle
Or a pint of beer,
But I should be used to that
As it happens every year.

Sometimes I spend new year
With girlfriends of mine,
And when it gets to midnight
We all sing Auld Lang Syne.

Other times I spend new year
With my very best friend,
We have a drink and a laugh
Until the very end.

When I'm with friends or family
They don't take the pee,
When I have my favourite drink
Which is WKD.

But it looks like this year
It will be such a bore,
As there are other requirements
Creating such a chore.

Christmas 2006

At first my Christmas savings club (Farepak)
Did go up the spout,
Leaving me at Christmas time
With absolutely nowt.

I then planned a night out with the girls
To do a Christmas shop.
But my alternator went
So that all had to stop.

I then had no hot water
Which took 7 weeks to do,
But with my landlord
That is nothing new.

Then my drive shaft went
On a very busy road,
Which most of my workmates blamed
On the very heavy load.

But at least I have my loved ones
Whom I truly do adore,
So when it comes to Christmas time
I could not ask for any more.

<u>Ding dong, Avon Manager</u>

For a while you were my manager
And the job you did was great,
But you have now retired
The bit that us reps hate.

You have jumped to help reps
In their time of need,
And even many ex reps
Have praised your good deed.

So next time I go 'ding dong'
I will be thinking "Thanks Jayne",
As without your help
My job would be a pain.

But you have now retired
So you can sit and rest,
As while doing Avon
You did your very best.

Ding Dong, Avon Manager 2

While I have done Avon
I have had a manager (or 2 or 3),
Some of them were helpful
And some never contacted me.

When I have had problems
And Avon caused me stress,
You have stepped in
And sorted out the mess.

You set up a page on Facebook
Just for Area 485,
Which helped us create friendships
And helped each other survive.

You arranged a Christmas party
ALMOST a girls' night out,
So we met each other
A crowd so lovely beyond doubt.

So I wish you good luck
In everything you do,
So this sends all the best
Just from me to you.

Mobile voicemail

Hi, Sorry I can't take your call
I may be on another phone,
Or I could just be tolerating
Hearing my ex moan.

I also may be driving
And we all know the law,
And with my experience
That point can be sore.

You can, however, try me
On another line,
Well you have loads to pick from
Any one of nine.

But I might have worked a night shift
And I could be asleep,
So please leave me a message
When you hear the beep.

Valentine's day – every year

Valentine's day comes and goes
And I spend it alone,
All I have for company
Is EVERY mobile phone.

I don't get a cuddle
Or a pint of beer,
But I should be used to that
As it happens every year.

My sister Jodi and her partner together eleven years

Eleven years have now passed
Since something really great,
When my sister Jodi
Went on a blind date.

The person who set this up
Did something very grand,
So I would like to meet them
And then shake their hand.

Jodi took on Sam
Like he was her own son,
And had 2 beautiful children
Which was a job so greatly done.

Rich is a Chef
And his cooking is so fine,
Well it is so much better
Than anything of mine.

Jodi qualified as a Beautician
Which she does outstandingly,
I will give you one example
Just take a look at me.

They both then got married
Which really made MY day,
As I had the honour
Of giving Jodi away.

So I would like to say "Thank you Rich"
As your relationship is so fine,
As I could not ask for anybody better
To be with a sister of mine.

So I will end this poem
With one last thing to say,
I am sending all my love and best wishes
Today and every day.

Why do I drive?

I worked on a Sunday night
And almost shed a tear,
As the only way I could get home
Was in second gear.

I then found out on the Monday
It could cost very much,
As the problem
Is the stupid clutch.

I then found out on the Tuesday
Some very nasty facts,
I only have another week
Before I renew my car tax.

I got a text on Wednesday night to say
We checked your car for sure,
We will ring you on Thursday
To let you know some more.

Thursday then arrived
And I was off to bed,
Instead of sitting and waiting
For that call instead.

Friday is the end of the week
And I hoped my car was done,
As I required that
To get my lovely son.

Then the weekend did hit us
And the problems (AGAIN) did start,
So sometimes I just wish
BRING BACK THE HORSE AND CART.

If I could turn back time

As this century has gone on
Not everything has worked out – of course,
At the start of the century
I had a messy divorce.

One good thing from my marriage
Was a baby that I held,
When the time came
And my son entered this world.

Ever since then
Things have not gone my way,
I have ended up alone
Every Valentine's day.

I would have had a better education
And a top class job,
To give me a classy future
Earning a few more bob.

But if I didn't have that education
There is one thing I could not mend,
I would never have ended up meeting
My very best friend.

I had some crappy Christmases
Which I am scared to look back,
And the hardest was when
I lost out to Farepak.

In 2012 I had surgery
Which left me in loads of pain,
So I just hope
I never have that again.

2013 was another poor Christmas
As a bar had hit me on the head,
Causing tooth damage
Meaning I needed implants instead.

One thing I would never change
Which really made me smile,
Was when I had the honour
Of walking my sister down the aisle.

For quite a while
Things have not been great,
I have eaten a few wrong things
And gained a little weight.

I am even getting old
Although my looks don't show,
I am getting closer
To that big four 0.

Despite one of my jobs
Not paying too well,
I will never regret
Meeting each Avon girl.

I have had nephews and nieces
All come my way,
Which has been great
In every single way.

So with so much bad
And not always being at my prime,
I still would not consider it
If I could TURN BACK TIME.

Approaching the big FOUR 0

Only 55 days to go
Until my party night,
When I am with those close to me
Sharing my delight.

Only thing that is bad
Which does make me moan,
Before the night arrives
I need to lose at least one stone.

But there is one thing
That I really must say,
Some of the girls want me
To dance the night away.

But when I go on the dance floor
It is not great for me,
As my sister will confirm
As she always takes the pee.

DJ, hall and invites
Have all been done,
With all the thanks
To my lovely mum.

I have a music idea
And 14 songs I want to hear,
But one thing I must avoid
Is drinking too much beer.

I really must behave
I really can't be naughty,
As I am approaching
The tender age of fourty.

But I must say most of all
The best thing of the night,
I will have all my friends and family
There within my sight.

Christmas 2014

Christmas is getting close
And I do have some fear,
As things go wrong at Christmas
Every single year,

Sometimes it is the car
Or the bank manager giving me grief,
Or a bar on my head
Knocking out my teeth.

Then my Christmas saving went
Because of collapsed Farepak,
Another finished in hospital
Because of my back.

This Christmas is already going wrong
With something to remove my smile,
I have just stepped on the scales
My heaviest for a long while.

So to avoid things going wrong
And to take away the fear,
I might just lock myself away
Until the new year.

40th birthday speech

I would like to say a massive 'Thank you'
To everybody here tonight,
For coming to my big FOUR 0
Although you would not realise by this handsome sight.

Exactly 40 years ago
An angel entered this world,
And that is a perfection
Which I have upheld.

I have become a brother
And a dad and so much more,
To such a loving family
Whom I do adore.

But we do have one very special person here
Who arranged all this and provided so many loving hours,
So I would like to thank my dear mum Trudy for everything
By giving her these flowers.

It's good to talk

When I was married
I had one phone,
Which made and took calls
So I couldn't moan.

I then got number two
With a great cashback deal,
And weekends were free
Which seemed so unreal.

Then when divorced
I got number three,
As peak calls cost nothing
And it helped me break free.

Then my careful driving
Was worth so much more,
I renewed my insurance
And they made it four.

Then my bill grew
As my texts did thrive,
So I got a text phone
And that made it five.

I then met a nice girl
And my bill played tricks,
So I joined her network
And that made it six.

Then one great company
Whom I represent,
Made my £15
Very well spent.

Avon Cosmetics
Made me feel in heaven,
As their fantastic offer
Then made it seven.

Then after a boot sale
With my very best friend,
I got phone number eight
And that WAS the end.

Then after a reunion with
Some old school friends of mine,
I got my last phone
And finished with nine.

BUT I then got an Ipad
Which is so great,
So I don't need all those phones
And I reduced it to eight.

Painful 2015

At home in pain
And it's agony to wash in the bath,
It even hurts my body
If I try to laugh.

I can't even catch up with my programs
As there is nowhere comfy for me,
It is even painful
If I try to have a pee.

I drive with a hot water bottle
As it helps a little with the pain,
But I finish the journey
And it hits me again.

I can not bend, stretch, sneeze or laugh
There is not much I can do,
As the worst thing right now
Is when I need a poo.

I might need surgery
But they don't know yet,
But with my luck in life
It is a likely bet.

But the good thing right here
And I don't know where I would be,
If it wasn't for the help and support
From friends and family.

A man's poem

She didn't like the plumbing
She didn't like the repair,
She said I was disrespectful
Not like how her father used to care.

I didn't do enough at home
She thought I didn't have a clue,
She thought I couldn't iron
Like her father used to do.

I then worked day and helped at night
Then took abuse all the way through,
Then recovered at work the next day
The way her father used to do.

A perfect facial

I see an ad online
And I had to look twice,
As I read something which
Seemed so very nice.

It offered a free facial
With feedback as the only request,
So the girls jumped for it
And the outcome was the best.

This might seem mad
But I cannot lie,
There was even a request
Made by one mad guy.

I must admit
That mad guy was me,
But I love looking after myself
And taking ageing so carefully.

I don't want to look old
Or even look a scruff,
Like you see with many blokes
Who look so very rough.

I really don't care
What other people say,
Some think my procedure
Can be rather gay.

But the facial that I had
Was the very best,
So I would recommend
It to all the rest.

A painful time

I can't sleep
I am feeling pain,
And my physio thinks
I could soon be working again.

Someone click a finger
And resolve it all,
As this pain stops me
Doing much at all.

I can't have fun
I can't do very much,
But thankfully I get around
With the use of my crutch.

This might sound odd
You might think I am a pain,
But I would much rather be
At work slaving again.

I will celebrate my recovery
Without a single doubt,
I will probably
Arrange a GIRL'S night out.

You might laugh
You might even take the pee,
But my girlfriends are a laugh
And something great for me.

Doctor's don't care

At home in pain
And bored in bed,
I'd rather be watching
Loose Women instead.

But there was nowhere I could sit
As I felt a mess,
Because when I was seated
The pain was in excess.

I had fourteen wires attached
To my handsome bulk,
Which helped with the pain
But made me want to sulk.

27 tablets a day
Lead me to feel sorrow,
I could almost open
My own chemist tomorrow.

Doctors didn't care
They didn't want to help me,
Even my physio was shocked
And thought they took the pee.

So I did just suffer
And hoped it got resolved soon,
As when it was sorted
I would be over the moon.

Unlucky century

As this century has gone on
Not much has gone right for me,
I had a messy divorce
And a landlord who takes the pee.

I lost money to Farepak
And had a bar hit me on the head,
That caused dental damage
But could have been brain damage instead.

I recovered from Farepak
But then it was the car,
Then I was hospitalised
So I could not get very far.

I then recovered from that
And (while in bed) heard a smash,
I then peeped out the window
And see my car received a crash.

To make things even worse
The person did not stay,
Which left me another bill
Just like every day.

That situation then improved
And things started to look up for me,
But then I wrote the car off on the A12
Which felt like tragedy.

I then replaced that car
Which went wrong from start to end,
But when it comes to driving
Cars are not my friend.

I then replaced that car again
And it was ok apart from a few 'buts',
The worst bit for me was
When someone tampered with my nuts.

I then got to work
And my walking was not at its best,
So I got sent straight home
As I could not work like the rest.

I saw doctors, physios and been in hospitals
And they still didn't know why,
But I am used to things going wrong
Which almost made me want to cry.

But there is one bit of luck
Right out there for me,
And that is my special
Friends and family.

Without all of them
I don't know what I'd do,
So I have to say THANK YOU
To everyone of you.

Newspaper publication

To all my friends and family
I have some lovely news,
If you read the Essex Chronicle
You can give me your views.

You may laugh a lot
When you read page 20,
But what you read
I always wanted for me.

I contacted many publishers
But they all took the pee,
They only wanted to help
If I had loads of money.

So hurry up and buy the paper
Which comes out today,
Then post on here
What it makes you say.

But please don't be nasty
Or think that I am sad,
As the contents of what you read
Makes me very glad.

New year 2011

New years eve is almost here
And I won't get very far,
Because for the 6th year running
I haven't got a car.

I will start at the beautician
So I look just right,
When I go out for new year
For most of the night.

But it should be a great night
Until the very end,
As I will be on a boys' night out
With my very best friend.

But I will then have to
Return to normality,
And sort the car
Which blew up on me.

It has messed up my weekend
And stopped from me seeing my son,
So I can't wait
Until the car is done.

But when the car is done
It won't be such a thrill,
As I will be clobbered
With the stupid bill.

But with these problems
I almost want to cry,
As it happens every Christmas
And I really don't know why.

Pre wedding planning

Only 7 weeks to go
And I will have one great smile,
When I take my beautiful sister's arm
And walk her down the aisle.

I can still remember
Like it was yesterday,
When Jodi asked the question
"Will you give me away"?

I will try my hardest
And do the best I can,
Just like Jodi would want
From her lovely brother Dan.

But the only thing I do fear
But won't be out of my reach,
Is when it comes to the bit
Where I have to give a speech.

The not so lucky year

2015 is well under way
And it started great for me,
I celebrated with the big FOUR 0
Although I don't look over twenty.

But I then had car problems
And that I had to change,
So all my finances
I had to rearrange.

I then got sent home from work
As I walked in with a limp,
The way I was walking
I probably looked a wimp.

Doctors couldn't decide what was wrong
Could be nerves, sciatica or worse,
But I am used to bad luck
As I think someone has a curse.

But this is a great diet
As it's painful to prepare a meal,
Even getting out of bed
Isn't such a thrill.

But I suppose
I really cannot moan,
As I have been lucky
And lost over a stone.

Now I have another problem
One that I can't mend,
There is a noise on the car
I think it's the track rod end.

Another problem has occurred
Which really takes the pee,
I am unable to
Start up my PC.

This feels like Christmas
With things going wrong until the end,
I just thank god for family
And every single friend.

The medical disaster

I went to a physio
And he was not over the moon,
He gave me a letter
And said "see your doctor soon".

I went to the doctor
And the receptionists had a read,
They asked me to return in the morning
As it's the doctor I did urgently need.

But last time they said that
I was sent for a scan,
And the hospital worked
As best as they can.

I just don't want the same operation
As last time it caused me so much pain,
But with my luck in life
I will have that again.

So much pain

At home in bed
And my leg was in pain,
Hoping that I didn't
Need surgery again.

Doctors were doing
The best they can,
So I sat back and waited
For results of my scan.

I was doing something
Which is better than swimming,
I was just watching
The latest LOOSE WOMEN.

I would rather be at work
Because this takes the pee
As the pain sometimes
Is agony for me.

I was only 5 weeks away
From a boys' weekend,
But I would look stupid on crutches
While out with each friend.

But this is normal
With the way things go wrong,
So I just suffered
For so very long.

But the good thing here
Which is great for me,
I know I always have
Those who are close to me.

2 weeks until 40

2 weeks until I'm surrounded
By friends and family,
Moments away from hitting
The tender age of 40.

I have another birthday on the Sunday
One that I can't miss,
Such a social weekend
So much better than this.

But I will be around
So many who do care,
I am still stuck
For what I should wear.

But I do know
The night will be great,
So I must admit
I REALLY CANNOT WAIT.

New year's greetings

Before the night get too late
And I drink too much red wine,
I would like to wish a happy new year
To all friends of mine.

If I touch too much red
I might get some stick,
When I drink too quick
And get a little sick.

So while I am with my best friend
I will stick to the beer,
But I wish everybody else
A very happy new year.

300 days before the big 40th

Only three hundred days
As I do well know,
Until I hit
The big FOUR 0.

I know I don't look over twenty
As I keep young and handsome also,
As everybody tells me
And I do well know.

I can't help looking so young
It just comes naturally,
Well that is what happens
As everybody tells me.

So I just need to keep young
And not let people get to me,
So I am still so handsome
When I hit fifty.

__Kerry__

Kerry claims to work hard
For the cash in her hand,
Making excuses for a watch
Costing several grand.

In one single month
Most don't get her sum,
We have to work much harder
To keep clothes on our bum.

I'm one example
With the two jobs I do,
A dairy by day
And takaways until I go 'phew'.

My divorce debts
I am trying to clear,
And earn for my children
Whom I love so dear.

With Dawn (my lovely girlfriend)
Our time is so rare,
Which makes Kerrys' income
Cause me to swear.

I'm just catching up with Loose Women
From 3 weeks ago,
As my work and my children
Make my catching up slow.

But I tape Loose Women
Each day of the week,
As I love all the gossip
The wit and the cheek.

After a car accident

It's a good job I'm not religious
With the way things go for me,
Because if there is someone up there
They really take the pee.

Things go wrong every Christmas
Often with the car,
Which prevents me
From getting very far.

But last Christmas was not too bad
Until we hit Jan,
Then it went wrong again
As much as it can.

Bosses don't care who I work with
Bank manager don't care about my life,
Which makes things seem as bad
As when I was with my ex wife.

I needed another bumper
As mine was hanging off the car,
But I couldn't get one
Without stretching money too far.

Even when I got one
I could not go far,
As it is something
I couldn't fit on the car

I used loads of tape on my bumper
Which looked fine to me,
But that did hang loose
Which really took the pee.

So I just suffered
But I always have those close to me,
As I really don't know where I'd be
Without friends and family.

New year's resolutions – The four F's

I'm going to sort my FINANCES
And improve my FLAT,
Also sort my FITNESS
And reduce my FAT.

Football season 2013

To all the Tottenham
Fans that I know,
I am sat here
With one big glow.

You are now 4th
With one game to go,
So on Sunday
The results will show.

Do not cry
Or get out of hand,
When you lose
To Sunderland.

It could be worse
So don't cry a tear,
As you might get
Religated one year.

A-Z – 26 new year's resolutions

I am going to be more ADVENTUROUS
And not be a BORE,
Keep CALM when people annoy me
And DECORATE my flat which is an eyesore.

I am going to sort my ELEGANCE
And sort my FITNESS also,
And get down the GYM
So my HEALTH does glow.

I will stay IMMACULATE
And as JOYFUL as can be,
Be KISSABLE for the girls
And get a LIFE for me.

I will make my life more MEANINGFUL
And stay very NEAT,
Also be more OUTGOING
And POSITIVE instead of defeat.

I am going to watch my QUIDS
And hopefully become RICH one day,
I will SWIM more
In TIME that comes my way.

I don't want to be UNFIT
I want to be VALUED in my job,
I also want to lose some WEIGHT
So I am not a fat slob.

I don't want to be XL
I want to be slim again,
I want to stay YOUNG at heart
And maybe do a bit of ZEN.

New year fun

New year's eve is almost here
And I can not wait,
As I will sing Auld Lang Syne
With my very best mate.

I will start the new year
Hopefully better for me,
As I started last year
Having surgery.

I'm just working out my resolutions
Which really must not fail,
Listing a whole A-Z
Which I'm working on right now.

But I do have
What's most important to me,
And that is having
My friends and family.

A day at a theme park

Last year I went with a friend
To visit Thorpe Park,
We had a great time
And stayed until dark.

I have a fear of heights
But my friend assured me well,
But the rides wrecked me
And Billie claimed I screamed like a girl.

I then went on a ride
And embarrassment was badly felt,
When they kicked me off
As they couldn't do the belt.

We had priority tickets
So we could jump each queue,
But once we were on
I had to grip like glue.

I thought my nerves were bad before
With so many nervous hours,
But I'm never going again
After the outcome at Alton Towers.

So next time a friend goes up London Shard
Or maybe London Eye,
I will sit and watch
And you will know why.

Santa fun run

December is getting closer
And there is one thing I can't miss,
Which will be the fun run
Which is for a local hospice.

I had my doubts about it
Because of my back surgery,
But this hospice have
Helped people close to me.

I may have to stop half way
And have a little pause,
When I do the fun run
Dressed as Santa Claus.

But I already have sponsors
So there is no dropping out,
So I will just go for it
And complete it without a doubt.

So I will thank everybody in advance
For sponsors they are doing or have done,
Because when it comes to Santa Claus
You know I am number one.

A poor 2012

2012 is near the end and I will be glad
When the memory is afar,
At the start of the year my cambelt went
So I didn't have a car.

I then ended up in hospital
And recovery took a while,
I even struggled to walk
Down the supermarket aisle.

While I was recovering
I got three tickets on my car,
One because of a breakdown
So I could not get very far.

Another ticket was not my fault
But it was a stupid risk,
I had not noticed a mess up
The Post Office made with my tax disc.

Then women kept moaning about my bulge
And many of them did nag,
So I felt obliged
To buy a man bag.

I then had another problem
Which messed things for me,
When I ended up
Blowing up my PC.

Then I didn't have a car again
Although it did seem fine,
As it appeared that
I had blown that engine of mine.

But there has been one good thing
Which has really helped me,
And that is the help and support
From friends and family.

Forced to 'HOPPIT'

I limped round a supermarket
But I didn't need that much,
I managed just right
With the help from my crutch.

I then went to get petrol
Which I needed for the car,
As I knew without it
I would not get very far.

I limped into the garage
Then back to the car,
But when I drove off
I didn't get very far.

I see blue lights behind me
Which wasn't such a thrill,
As I got pulled over
By the old bill.

The police told me they were tipped off
That I couldn't walk very far,
Someone had told them
I was staggering to the car.

They breathalysed me
And that did not show much,
I even showed the evidence
As I stood there on the crutch.

So I would like to say "THANK YOU"
To the person who made the call,
As it left me in pain
And also look a fool.

A boys' weekend

Next weekend is getting closer
And I look forward to it very much,
Even though I will only get around
With the use of a crutch.

A school reunion
But I won't get far,
While the boys get drunk
At every single bar.

I will hobble along
With my tablets in tow,
As the NHS aren't helping
As I do well know.

But regardless of the pain
I will enjoy it until it ends,
As I will be on a reunion
With many old school friends.

A traffic warden's funeral

The traffic warden was lowered
Into the ground,
It started quietly
Without a single sound.

Then there was a noise
Which made them think instead,
They realised that
The warden might not be dead.

Then there was a bang
And a loud shout,
The warden screamed
"I'm not dead, LET ME OUT".

But the vicar smiled
And knew he had won,
So he commented sweetly
"Sorry, the paperwork is done".

School reunion 2015

A boys' weekend
Which is not far,
But with my medication
I will have to stay sober.

It will be a laugh
But I can't do much,
As every step
Will need a crutch.

While they drink beer
I will stick to coke,
The fluid type
As I am not that sort of bloke.

The first bit of the weekend
Won't be such a thrill,
As it involves walking
Up a steep hill.

But I must admit that hill
Is too much for me,
So I might have to do 500 yards
In a taxi.

But I don't care as I will laugh
Until the very end,
As I will be spending time
With each old school friend.

But my return
Won't be good for me,
As I will then find out
If I need surgery.

The surgery is something
I can't ignore,
As it was seriously
Painful before.

They cut me open
At the rear,
And the suffering
Was so clear.

So can someone close
Do one thing good for me,
Just hurry up and win
The bloody lottery.

My girlie friends and family

I got sent home from work
As walking was hard for me,
And straight away I had help
From my family.

Girl friends offered help
And ran around for me,
Some took me out
And others were so friendly.

The girls showed they cared
Family were a gem,
I don't know what I would have done
Without any of them.

I got messages on Facebook
And texts to ONE phone,
Which showed so much care
So I cannot moan.

I might recover with injections
But it's a weirdness I can not hide,
As the consultant told me
Its just a small prick in my backside.

But I don't care
What they have to do,
As I always know
I still got EVERYONE OF YOU.

FA Cup final 2015

I am at home
Having such a thrill,
As Arsenal have
Just made it 2-0.

Nothing on this earth
Will override my pain,
But it will give me smiles
If Arsenal score again.

We did better than Tottenham
And also West Ham too,
But that is expected
As we know what to do.

Walcott scored the first goal
Sanchez then scored number 2,
As we are the only team
Who know what to do.

So I must say sorry
To all the rest,
As you know Arsenal
ARE THE VERY BEST.

Mertesacker made me change the poem
With another thrill,
As he then made it
A MASSIVE 3-0.

But Giroud was not happy
3-0 was not enough for the best,
So he scored a goal
To confirm beating the rest.

Can't do much

Lying in bed
Feeling so sad,
Only thing I could do
Was the TV and ipad.

I had pains
That I really couldn't hide,
They were running
Down my right side.

Sometimes I felt fine
And didn't feel my pain much,
Other times I couldn't move
Without my crutch.

NHS were doing
The best they can,
They sent me for
My MRI scan.

I had a school reunion
The following weekend,
But I felt useless
While with each friend.

Doctors reckoned 2 weeks
For my MRI result,
But with my luck
Result was an insult.

With my luck in life
I didn't feel much hope,
Maybe I should become religious
And visit a Pope.

But I always had what's best
So I couldn't take the pee,
I always have everybody
Who is close to me.

When I recovered
I didn't have a doubt,
I had to arrange
A GIRL'S night out.

So anyone religious
I have one thing to say,
Just get on your knees
And start to prey.

Actually forget it
As it won't go my way,
Because bad luck is normal
For me every day.

A sleepless night

In bed, couldn't sleep
Suffering again,
My whole right side
Was in pain.

Instead of pain
I'd rather something instead,
Just the ability to
Fall asleep in bed.

My work provided
Loads of care,
Providing medical help
Absolutely everywhere.

NHS were crap
Doing little for me,
The waits I had
Really took the pee.

But family are great
And always there,
So nice to have
A family who care.

Girl friends were great
As I do well know,
They dragged me out
To play bingo.

But the other times
Were not the best,
As I had to spend so much time
Having a rest.

But then I do have
Absolutely no surprise,
As the physio insisted
Plenty of exercise.

So while I was at home
And bored in bed,
I thought I would write
This poem instead.

So now the poem is done
I felt I could weep,
As I then laid down
And tried to get some sleep.

A-Z of my life

A is for ACTIVE
Which I try to be,
By working so hard
And enjoying friends socially.

B is for BRAINTREE
The home town for me,
Where I met nice friends
Who are so lovely.

C is for CARING
Which I try to show every day,
To my friends and family
Whom send care my way.

D is for DAD
Which I would never hide,
As that is a title
Which gives me much pride.

E is for EMOTIONAL
Which I can sometimes be,
But that's because I care for
Those close to me.

F is for FAMILY
Whom mean so much,
Without them I would
Feel out of touch.

G is for GIRL FRIENDS
Whom truly do care,
When there are problems
You know they are there.

H is for HANDSOME
Which is me throughout,
I am just so good looking
Beyond all doubt.

I is for INTELLIGENT
Which comes naturally,
Well I do have a brain
With some accountancy.

J is for JOYFUL
Which is always me,
But that is thanks to
Such good friends and family.

K is for KIND
Which I always try to be,
Putting others first
Instead of me.

L is for LUCK
But I should miss that bit out,
Because my luck in life
Is often so poor without doubt.

M is for MARVELLOUS
Which is me all through,
Without my brains
What would you do?

N is for NUTTY
Which some claim is me,
But everything I do
Is done innocently.

O is for OSTEOPATH
Whom I often see,
They mess with my body
To reduce agony.

P is for POETRY
Which I find a thrill.
I can't help having
Such a good skill.

Q is for QUIET
Which some claim is me,
But I don't know why
As I can laugh quite loudly.

R is for RELIABLE
Which is me all through,
I never let people down
In the things that I do.

S is for SANTA
Which I do one week a year,
It's just for the laughs
Let me make that clear.

T is for TALENTED
That truly is me,
As explained already
With all my poetry.

U is for UNDERSTANDING
Which I make very clear,
When friends have problems
I always lend my ear.

V is for VALUABLE
Which I can't help be,
What would everyone do
If they didn't have me.

W is for WORK
As I always had a job,
I could never be
A dole scrounging slob.

X is for XENIAL
As I help everyone I can,
I just can't help being
Such a lovely man.

Y is for YOUTHFUL
Because of my handsome way,
I can't help looking younger
Every single day.

Z is for ZEALOUS
Which is me all through,
As I am devoted
In all that I do.

True friends

At home and bored
And gone berserk,
Almost wished that
I was at work.

It's took ages
And I felt a mess,
Because of such a wait
With the NHS.

Friends were active
And kept in touch,
Family were caring
Which meant so very much.

I kept in touch with
Most friends of mine,
By various ways
Mainly online.

I visited some friends
Others took me out,
Which meant so much
Without a single doubt.

So to you great friends
That show so much care,
If you ever need help
I WILL ALWAYS BE THERE.

Brother-in-law 40th

A time has arrived
One I can't ignore,
The big 40th
Of my brother-in-law.

I would not say you were 40
I could not say that,
With the way you look
I thought you were older than that.

Well I tried to be polite
I tried the best I can,
But I couldn't do better
For a Tottenham fan.

Now you are 40
You might not be such a fool,
You might see some sense
And support ARSENAL.

But despite your team
Doing worse than the rest,
Have a great 40th
And I wish you all the best.

AND

I know some of this card
Does really take the pee,
But I truly wish you all the best
And that comes from me.

I am sorry for the insults
I did the best I can,
But what else do you expect
From a brother-in-law like Dan.

Sister's poem of thanks

As I am sure you know
The last 6 months have been crap for me,
In and out of hospital
Been a physical tragedy.

It could have been worse
But you helped with the nasty facts,
You helped my machines work
By doing the leg wax.

I didn't enjoy the waxing
As it caused more pain,
I hope I never need
To have that again.

But I am glad you did it
As it helped in every way,
And even got the kids excited
And really made their day.

There was a good reason for it
As I know so much,
It helped towards my recovery
And helped put me back in touch.

Thanks to your help I can go back to work
Just part time for sure,
But my only other choice is
Sit at home in a bore.

Thanks to you and your help
It helped sort life for me,
Well at least until Christmas
As that occasion always takes the pee.

But I really must admit
I don't know where I would be,
Without the help and support
From such a loving family.

So there is one last thing
That I really must do,
And that is to say
A massive THANK YOU

Mum's poem of thanks

Over the past 6 months
Things have not been great for me,
In and out of hospital
And the car breaking down on me.

You have been there throughout
And helped all the way through,
Without your special help
I don't know what I would do.

You have been my new bank manager
And helped so very much,
Without all that help
My life would be out of touch.

But you have ALWAYS been there
Been much more than a mum can be,
From day one you have
Always supported me.

So for your help this year
And the love you have shown day to day,
I have to say a MASSIVE thank you
And send my love your way.

Grandmother's poem of thanks

Over the last 6 months
Things have not been great,
In and out of hospital
Which put me in a state.

On 2 different occasions
You helped and supported me,
While I was at yours
You gave me some money.

I appreciate the help you gave
In what you did do,
Which is why I sent this poem
As a way to say 'Thank you'.

That money helped with every day living
It helped me keep in touch,
So I have one last thing to say
And that is "THANK YOU VERY MUCH".

A friend's poem of thanks

Over the last 6 months
Things have been crap for me,
In and out of hospital
Risking surgery.

I was preparing myself
As I had to - just in case,
As my luck is low
And feels like a kick in the face.

But there are some people
Whom are always there,
Provide help when needed
And show they do care.

They have a magic touch
As it seems they know,
They turn themselves
Into a magical physio.

They provide some laughs
And don't take the pee,
When friends are at their poorest
They provide a private bingo taxi.

Despite thinking their friend's pain
Is sometimes a little fake,
They become a magical physio
And make a beautiful cake.

So when I go back to work
I look forward to a night of rest,
As when it comes to bingo fun
You truly are the best.

Christmas 2015

As this year has gone on
Not much has worked out by far,
At the start of the year
I had to replace my car.

But things then improved
So greatly for me,
I celebrated the big four 0
With friends and family.

Things then went downhill
And I could not do much,
As the only way I could get around
Was with the help from a crutch.

Then my wonderful sister
Taught me some nasty facts,
Never again in my life
Will I have a leg wax.

That same lovely sister
Stopped me looking a fool,
She then run me about
When I went into hospital.

The recovery was awkard
And something I could not hide,
As I had a 3 foot needle
Shoved in my backside.

I must admit that family
Really were a gem,
I don't know what I would have done
Without any of them.

One special person arranged my 40th
And has helped me all the way through,
Without that special person
I don't know what I would do.

That same special person helped so much
And gave my life a lift,
So I would like to thank my dear mum
With this little gift.

Printed in Great Britain
by Amazon.co.uk, Ltd.,
Marston Gate.